DoGi

a production of
DoGi, Firenze, Italia

Backpack Books
122 Fifth Avenue
New York, NY 10011

ISBN 0-7607-6971-0

Printed and bound in Italy

05 06 07 08 09 MCH 10 9 8 7 6 5 4 3 2 1

Library of Congress Cataloging-in-Publication Data
available upon request.

original title
Guarda dentro l'Egitto dei faraoni

text
Andrea Bachini (reference)
Rosaria Parretti (short stories)

illustrations
MM Comunicazione
(M. Cappon, M. Favilli, G. Sbragi, C. Scutti)

translation
Miranda MacPhail

games
Spartaco Albertarelli

graphic design and layout
Sansai Zappini

CREDITS
The illustrations were created through a project developed by
Eurolitho SpA–Divisione DoGi, copyright owner.
ILLUSTRATIONS
All illustrations in this book by
MM Comunicazione except for
p. 28 (Sebastiano Ranchetti) and p. 29 (Sergio).
REPRODUCTIONS
p. 29, Foto Siliotti

SEE INSIDE ANCIENT EGYPT

THE NILE'S GIFT

The Nile river forms a ribbon of water that crosses the North African deserts before separating into smaller branches and emptying into the Mediterranean Sea. It is the longest river in the world: the map here shows only the last 750 miles as it winds through the Nile valley and delta, the part that runs through Egypt.

The Nile played a fundamental role in the development of one of the most ancient civilizations in the world, the ancient Egyptian culture, which originated some 5,000 years ago. Back then, the banks of the river formed an area that the ancient Egyptians called the Black Lands because the soil was darkened by sediments deposited by the Nile's annual floods.

This narrow strip of fertile land bordered, to the east and west, the Red Lands, which were arid and desert-like. Every year the Nile waters overflowed their banks and brought new fertile soil to the Egyptian people.

Thanks to the great river, farming flourished so much that the Nile valley and its delta seemed like one vast farm. It was, however, the farmers' backbreaking labor that made the most of the opportunities presented by the river.

Farmers' work was regulated by the harsh discipline imposed by an absolute leader, the pharaoh, who was considered the intermediary between the human world and divine realms.

Memphis and the Giza pyramids

Memphis was the capital of ancient Egypt during the first period of its history, known as the Old Kingdom. Today at Giza, near Memphis, one can still see three great pyramids built 4,500 years ago as tombs for the pharaohs. Memphis was built on the Nile's west bank, near the delta. Not far away is the present-day capital of Egypt: Cairo.

LIBYAN DESERT

Cataracts and the Aswan Dam

The Nile used to have many cataracts, or drops in the level of the riverbed. The last one was near Aswan, on the southern border of ancient Egypt during its early history. In our modern era, in 1970, a dam was built here to hold back the Nile and form the great Nasser Lake. The huge Aswan Dam put an end to annual river flooding.

The Nile

The river flows for over 4,000 miles from its source to its delta. It receives water from the Sudan's White Nile (which in turn is fed by the great equatorial lakes) as well as from the Blue Nile (fed by rains on the far-off Ethiopian plateau). In the Egyptian valley, the Nile reaches a median width of almost 3,000 feet.

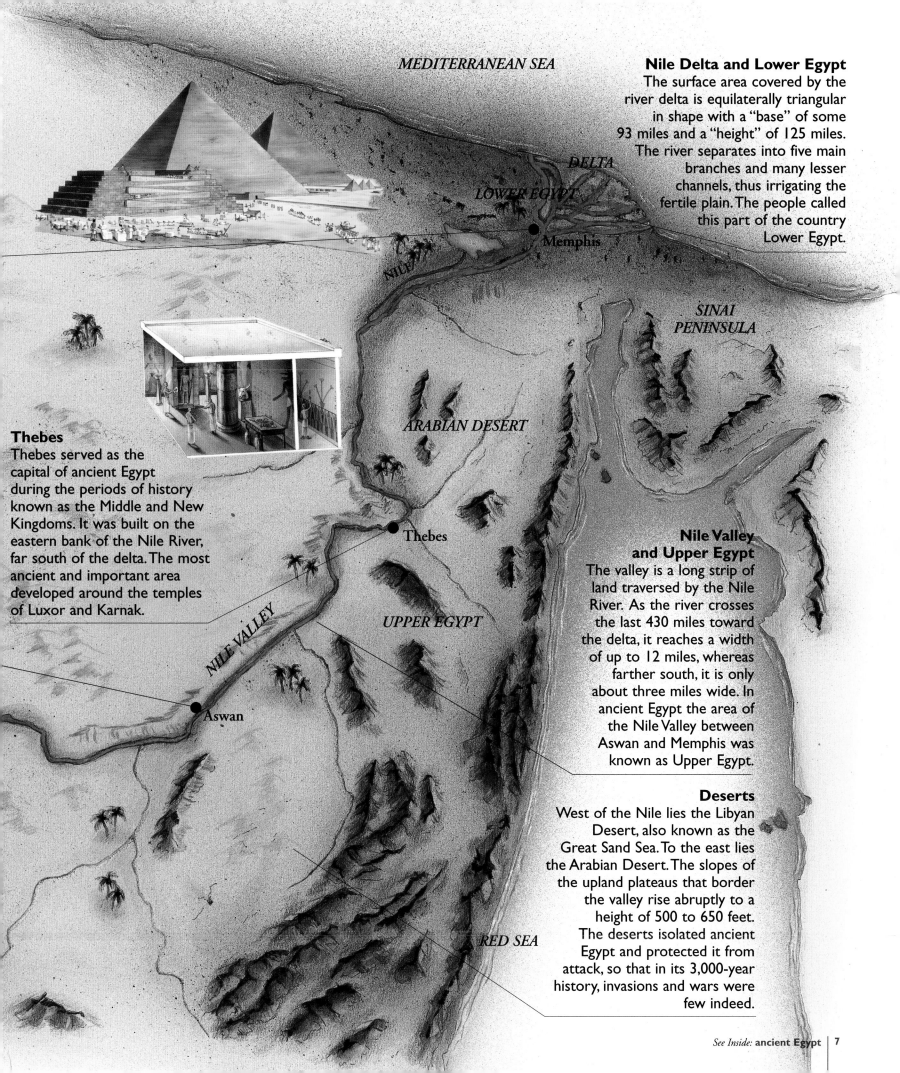

MEDITERRANEAN SEA

DELTA

LOWER EGYPT

Memphis

NILE

SINAI
PENINSULA

ARABIAN DESERT

Thebes

NILE VALLEY

UPPER EGYPT

Aswan

RED SEA

Nile Delta and Lower Egypt
The surface area covered by the river delta is equilaterally triangular in shape with a "base" of some 93 miles and a "height" of 125 miles. The river separates into five main branches and many lesser channels, thus irrigating the fertile plain. The people called this part of the country Lower Egypt.

Thebes
Thebes served as the capital of ancient Egypt during the periods of history known as the Middle and New Kingdoms. It was built on the eastern bank of the Nile River, far south of the delta. The most ancient and important area developed around the temples of Luxor and Karnak.

Nile Valley and Upper Egypt
The valley is a long strip of land traversed by the Nile River. As the river crosses the last 430 miles toward the delta, it reaches a width of up to 12 miles, whereas farther south, it is only about three miles wide. In ancient Egypt the area of the Nile Valley between Aswan and Memphis was known as Upper Egypt.

Deserts
West of the Nile lies the Libyan Desert, also known as the Great Sand Sea. To the east lies the Arabian Desert. The slopes of the upland plateaus that border the valley rise abruptly to a height of 500 to 650 feet. The deserts isolated ancient Egypt and protected it from attack, so that in its 3,000-year history, invasions and wars were few indeed.

THE THREE SEASONS

Life in Egypt was organized according to the cycles of the Nile River. Regular annual flooding and drought formed the basis of farm life and of the official calendar, which was divided into three seasons of four months each.

Akhet, or "time of flooding"
The first season in the Egyptian calendar began when the Nile flooded (around July 19) and ended in late autumn.

Peret, or "time of emergence"
Between mid-November and mid-March the level of the water went down, allowing farmers to cultivate the fields.

Papyrus
Found throughout Egypt, this plant was harvested in the season of *peret*. The reeds were first cut into narrow strips, then woven and pressed to obtain a resistant surface that could be used as writing paper.

Shemu, or "time of drought"
Between mid-March and mid-July, the Nile waters reached their lowest levels. This was the period for reaping and threshing wheat as well as for harvesting grapes.

Farmers
The majority of the ancient Egyptian population was made up of farmers. In spite of their exhausting and endless labor, they were barely able to make a living.

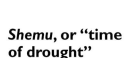

Papyrus boats
Lightweight and easily handled, these were used for harpoon fishing and hunting.

The Great River

Finally the day had come and Sneferu couldn't stand the wait any longer. When his father had made the promise, he had also said, "You must wait till the season of *akhet* comes and the flooding begins." And on that very day, at dawn, Sirius the morning star had once again appeared on the horizon, after an absence of 70 days. It was visible for a mere instant before the sun began to rise. For everyone it was the sign marking the beginning of the season of *akhet* and of the new year. Now it was up to the river: in a day or two it would begin to swell and flood the fields. In this way the god Hapi would bless the land with his gifts and with his life-giving, fertile strength.

But for little Sneferu the arrival of *akhet* coincided that year with something very special that didn't have much to do with the change of seasons or with the fertility of farmland soil. For Sneferu, *akhet* meant departure and the beginning of fantastic adventures. His father had resolved to embark on a new trip, and for the first time, Sneferu would accompany him. At long last he would travel with his father down the great river on a felucca!

In fact, the river was an incredible means of transport that reached into the very heart of vast territories, many of them still unexplored. *Akhet* was the best time of year to ply the waters, either with large ships or smaller feluccas, using that majestic road to carry people, goods, and materials of all kinds and all weights—even gigantic obelisks carved in stone!

Sneferu's father had already navigated his felucca along the river many times. He had gone as far as Nubia, called the "Land of the Bow" for its famous archers. He had always returned with fabulous gold necklaces and bracelets, objects carved in ivory and ebony, the priceless hides of animals never seen before, precious perfumes. . . . In this way he had built up his fortune and now enjoyed some prestige among the household of the royal family. Sneferu's father often boasted of having been personally admitted to the pharaoh's presence and of having made a special gift to the royal family!

It had happened that on his way back from a trip once, he had brought a dancer from one of the far-off populations, the Pygmies. He had made a gift of the Pygmy to the pharaoh, who was so delighted that he had had his scribe write a message of thanks. Sneferu still had a clear memory of the day the royal messenger had come to their house with the papyrus scroll. His father had been very struck by that gesture. Who knows—maybe Sneferu, too, would bring something back from his trip exotic enough to give the pharaoh.

"Are we going to hunt hippopotamuses, too?" asked Sneferu, very excited at the thought.

"If they leave our felucca alone, there won't be any need to kill them. Even so, there will be lots of excitement."

You, too, can travel down the Nile—just turn the page!

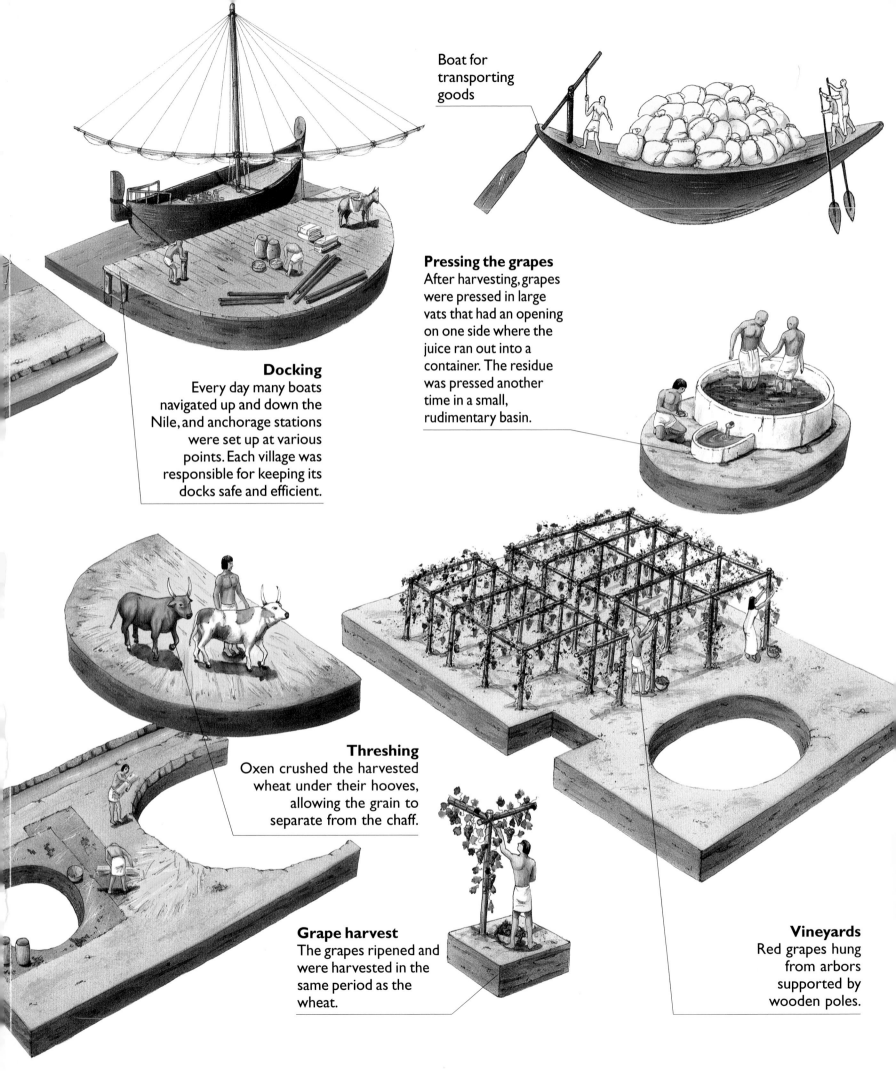

Boat for transporting goods

Pressing the grapes
After harvesting, grapes were pressed in large vats that had an opening on one side where the juice ran out into a container. The residue was pressed another time in a small, rudimentary basin.

Docking
Every day many boats navigated up and down the Nile, and anchorage stations were set up at various points. Each village was responsible for keeping its docks safe and efficient.

Threshing
Oxen crushed the harvested wheat under their hooves, allowing the grain to separate from the chaff.

Grape harvest
The grapes ripened and were harvested in the same period as the wheat.

Vineyards
Red grapes hung from arbors supported by wooden poles.

Shaduf

Egyptians raised water from wells or from the river to fill their irrigation canals. To achieve this, they used a device, still in use today, known as a *shaduf*: a long pole that rises and falls, with one end tied to a large bucket and the other to a counterweight.

Hydraulic works

Farmers built levees to control the effects of overflooding. They dug basin areas to store water as well as channels to take any runoff to irrigate areas untouched by the high waters.

Growing papyrus

Papyrus farming was very common in ancient Egypt. In pre-dynastic times (that is, before the reign of the pharaohs), bundles of papyrus reeds were tied together to build boats.

Hunting hippos

Hippopotamuses could disrupt river navigation and destroy crops, so they were often hunted as game.

Trawl fishing

This method was practiced especially during the Old Kingdom. The trawl was spread in shallow waters where the fishermen could walk, dragging the large net along with them.

Donkeys

Even today nomadic tribes and oasis dwellers prefer this animal above all others for doing basic, everyday chores.

Harvesting

Using wooden scythes with flint blades, farmers cut the wheat at knee height, then gathered it into stacks. The grain was piled into large baskets and loaded on donkeys.

Silos

Built on bases of dried mud, these round constructions had a small window at the top and another at the bottom.

Farmers sifting wheat

THE DRY SEASON

During *shemu*, the last season of the year, work in the fields reached a feverish pitch. All the crops had to be harvested before the next flood. It was also the time to build and repair banks, dams, and canals in order to avoid damage from violent flood-waters. Such works also allowed better usage of the water resources in case flooding proved less abundant than usual.

Grain warehouses
After harvesting, farmers stowed the grain away. Every farmer had to pay a tribute to the pharaoh either in grain, meat, flax, papyrus, or another material. The amount was calculated according to how much land was planted by the farmer's village and whether he owned livestock, fruit trees, or reed beds.

Nile's riches

The Nile was the only means of communication in ancient Egypt. Moreover, the river habitat produced beautiful flora, like papyrus, water lilies, lotuses, reeds, and acacias as well as a variety of fauna: hippopotamuses, crocodiles, antelopes, gazelles, marsh birds, and many kinds of fish.

Villages

Groups of dwellings were situated near the farmed fields and alongside the river or its canals. Made of rough bricks and plaster, the houses were arranged in rows. Front doors provided the only light and ventilation.

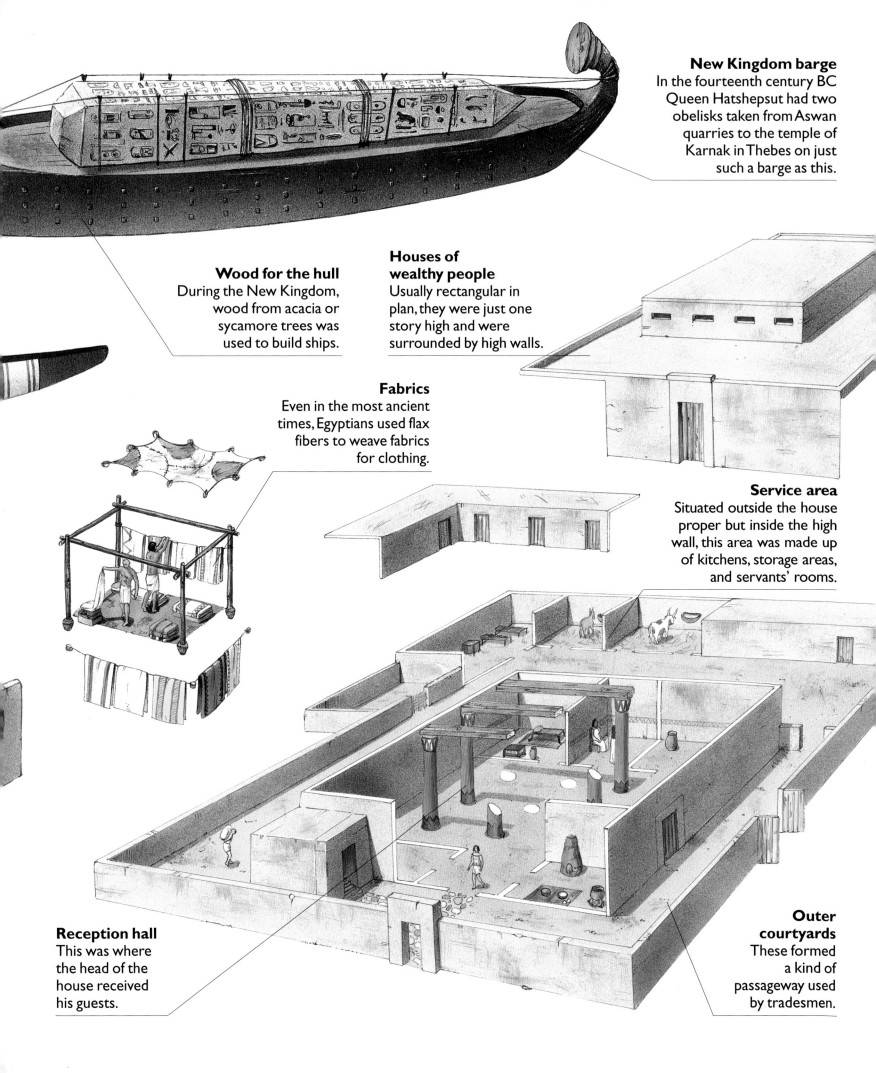

New Kingdom barge
In the fourteenth century BC Queen Hatshepsut had two obelisks taken from Aswan quarries to the temple of Karnak in Thebes on just such a barge as this.

Wood for the hull
During the New Kingdom, wood from acacia or sycamore trees was used to build ships.

Houses of wealthy people
Usually rectangular in plan, they were just one story high and were surrounded by high walls.

Fabrics
Even in the most ancient times, Egyptians used flax fibers to weave fabrics for clothing.

Service area
Situated outside the house proper but inside the high wall, this area was made up of kitchens, storage areas, and servants' rooms.

Reception hall
This was where the head of the house received his guests.

Outer courtyards
These formed a kind of passageway used by tradesmen.

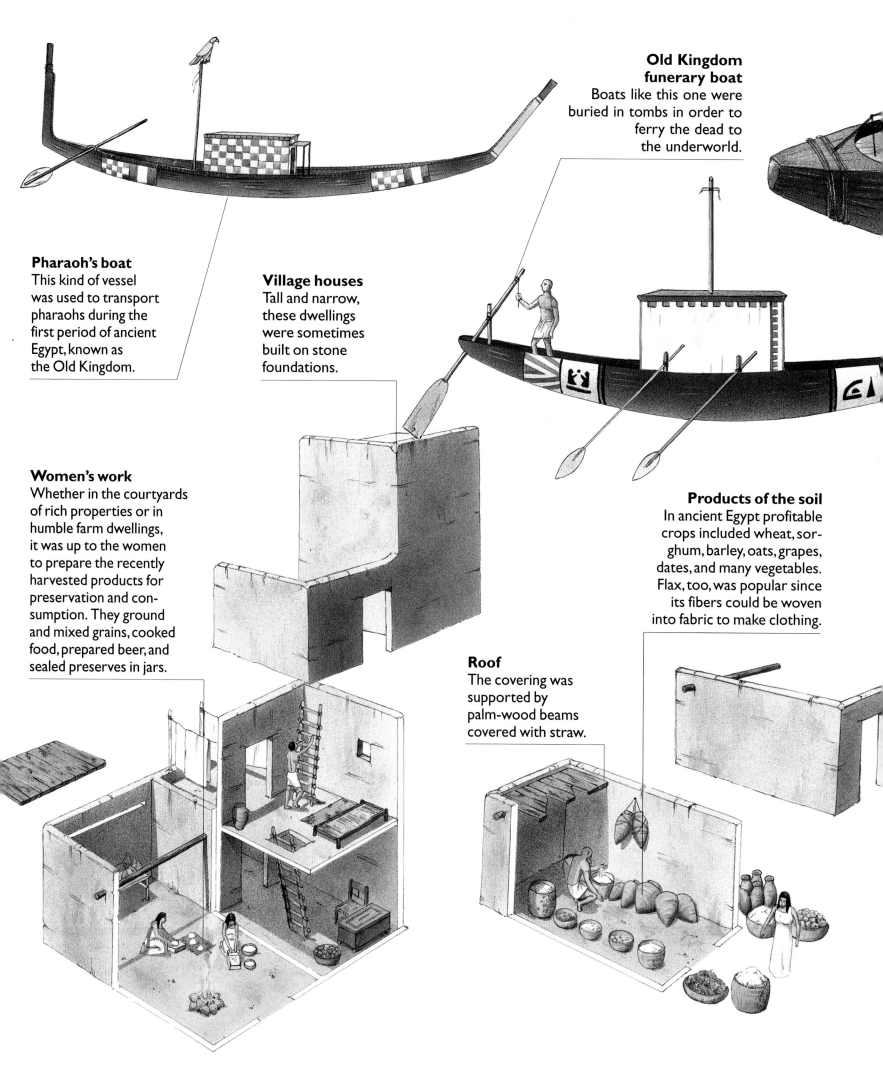

Old Kingdom funerary boat
Boats like this one were buried in tombs in order to ferry the dead to the underworld.

Pharaoh's boat
This kind of vessel was used to transport pharaohs during the first period of ancient Egypt, known as the Old Kingdom.

Village houses
Tall and narrow, these dwellings were sometimes built on stone foundations.

Women's work
Whether in the courtyards of rich properties or in humble farm dwellings, it was up to the women to prepare the recently harvested products for preservation and consumption. They ground and mixed grains, cooked food, prepared beer, and sealed preserves in jars.

Products of the soil
In ancient Egypt profitable crops included wheat, sorghum, barley, oats, grapes, dates, and many vegetables. Flax, too, was popular since its fibers could be woven into fabric to make clothing.

Roof
The covering was supported by palm-wood beams covered with straw.

THE NILE FLOODS

For 2 players

Object of the game:
To irrigate your fields before the other player

You will need:
2 dice
9 coins for each player

How to play:
The player who best imitates a pharaoh's pose, facial expression, or clothing begins the game.

One player plays on the left side of the Nile River while the other plays on the right. On his or her turn each player must roll the dice to try to bring floodwaters to one of the nine plowed fields on his or her side of the river. The player can use the total obtained from both dice or can use them individually to cover with one or two coins the plowed fields that are still unmarked.

For example: If on his or her first turn, a player rolls a 6 and a 3, that player can choose to put a coin on the plowed field number 9 (6 + 3) or else two coins on the fields numbered 3 and 6.

On each field there can only be one coin at a time. Each player can only roll once per turn.

End of the game:
The game goes on until one player succeeds in putting a coin on every one of the nine plowed fields on his or her side of the river.

Player 1 Left Bank		Player 2 Right Bank
1		1
2		2
3		3
4		4
5		5
6		6
7		7
8		8
9		9

Khufu's Pyramid

The three pyramids in Giza are true wonders, and people from all over the world come to admire them. The area is always full of tourists of every race and persuasion, all speaking their different languages.

Today, among the great multitude of people, Nino and his sister, Meli, are accompanied by their parents. Both children have always been fascinated by the mysteries of these enigmatic buildings. And now in front of Khufu's pyramid, they hope, at last, to learn some more.

However, what their mother reads out loud on page 143 of the guidebook doesn't satisfy their curiosity. "Built on an area of 5.3 acres, Khufu's pyramid soars some 480 feet in height and is made from two and a half milion blocks of limestone, each weighing over two tons. . . ."

But at this point a strange individual, dressed in a thin robe of white cloth and a bizarre kind of headdress, comes forward and interrupts the reading.

"The guides," he says, "never give the most interesting information."

What a deep voice! It immediately captures Nino and Meli's attention, and they are fascinated by this stranger. It seems he may know some great secrets.

"What do you know about the secrets of these pyramids' construction?" Meli blurts out.

"They took about 30 years of hard work by some 25,000 people such as bricklayers, stone cutters, ramp constructors, and tool builders," the man answers as if he were reading from a book.

Nino, a little disappointed with the stranger's answer, asks, "What about the theory that says that the position of the three pyramids recalls the orientation of the stars in the constellation of Orion?"

"When construction on my pyramid began, I didn't know where they would site the other two pyramids. You should ask Khepri and Menkaura. . . ."

"YOUR pyramid?"

"Yes, my pyramid, the tallest one! I still remember clearly how we began this massive work. We had to solve problems that seemed unsurmountable. . . . But they managed to make it just the way I wanted. With the room excavated in the rock under the monument, the passageway to the queen's chamber, the steep Grand Gallery that leads to the king's chamber, the room where my sarcophagus was placed. . . ."

Nino, Meli, Mommy, and Daddy are all dumbstruck and cannot believe their ears: "But who are you?"

"I am the second pharaoh of the fourth of the thirty dynasties that ruled over Egypt. I am Khufu."

"Good Lord, it's a mummy! . . ."

"No, my mummy is in a secret place. Otherwise, if my body were not well preserved, I would not be able to spend eternity in the company of the gods, together with Ra the sun god. And today is really a lovely sunny day–don't you think so?"

Oh, yes, at Giza you can really meet the strangest people. But now it's time to turn the page and discover the secrets of the Great Pyramid!

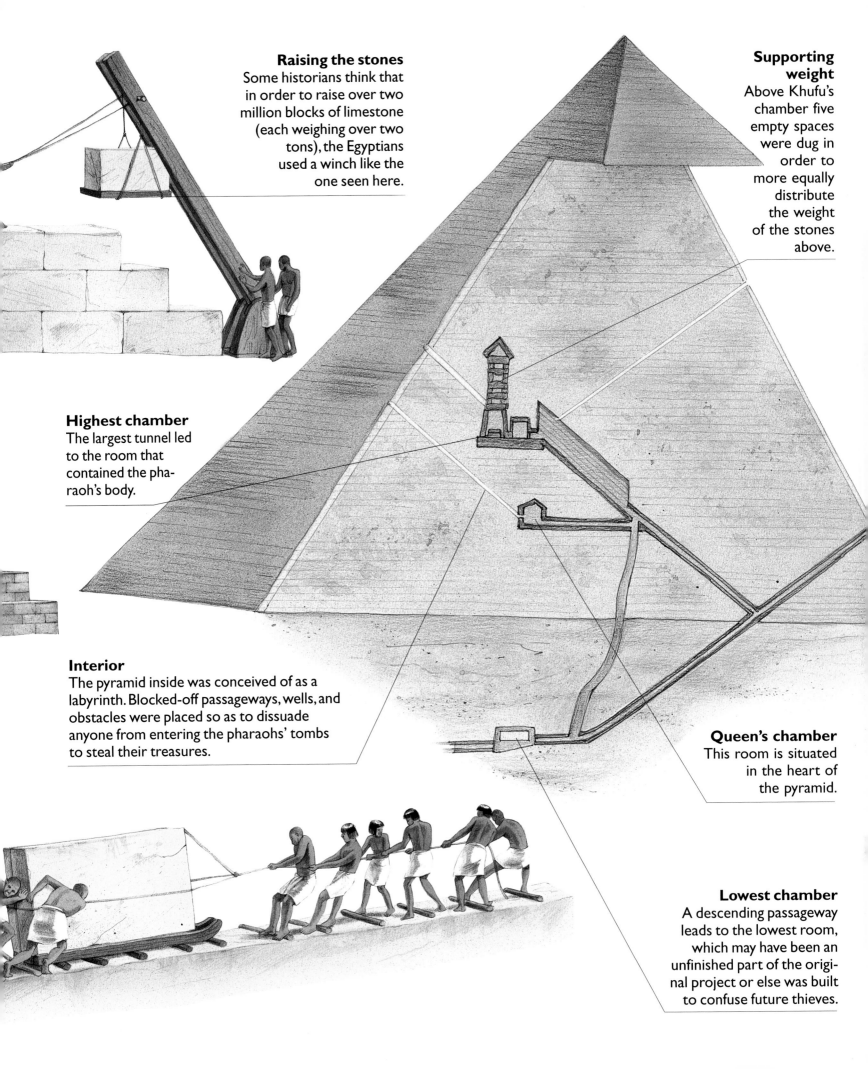

Raising the stones
Some historians think that in order to raise over two million blocks of limestone (each weighing over two tons), the Egyptians used a winch like the one seen here.

Supporting weight
Above Khufu's chamber five empty spaces were dug in order to more equally distribute the weight of the stones above.

Highest chamber
The largest tunnel led to the room that contained the pharaoh's body.

Interior
The pyramid inside was conceived of as a labyrinth. Blocked-off passageways, wells, and obstacles were placed so as to dissuade anyone from entering the pharaohs' tombs to steal their treasures.

Queen's chamber
This room is situated in the heart of the pyramid.

Lowest chamber
A descending passageway leads to the lowest room, which may have been an unfinished part of the original project or else was built to confuse future thieves.

Bricklayers

There weren't many specialized artisans who could work year-round on building the pyramids. For the most part the bricklayers were farmers from villages, drafted into constructing the pyramids during the flooding season, when it was impossible to work the fields.

Assembly line

All operations (from quarrying and shipping the stone to shaping and mounting it) were organized as a kind of "assembly line" in order to avoid bottlenecks and long waits.

Ramps

To build up the pyramid, workers may have used great ascending ramps that zigzagged up the side. The enormous square blocks would then have been dragged up with the help of sleds. Some scholars believe that although the ramps' moderate incline was well suited to the job of facing the outside surface, it was not useful for the actual construction.

Stones

The pyramids were mostly built from limestone, whereas the interior corridors and rooms were faced with granite. Sculptures were usually carved in sandstone, which is harder than limestone but easier to work than granite.

Menkaura's quarry

These stone blocks, quarried in Aswan, were transported some 1,300 miles across the whole of Upper Egypt.

Multitude of workers

The Greek historian Herodotus wrote that building a pyramid took 20 years for 1,000 men working in three-month shifts.

Moving stones

Transported via the Nile, the blocks were then dragged on wooden sleds over rollers before being finally raised into place.

THE PYRAMIDS

Since the beginning of the Egyptian era, the tombs of pharaohs and high functionaries symbolized the power these men enjoyed while they were still alive. During the Third Dynasty of pharaohs, tombs also became symbols of the king's divine status. Around the middle of the third millennium BC, pharaohs' tombs were constructed in the form of perfect pyramids, like the famous ones in Giza. Today this site, near the ancient capital of Memphis and the present-day capital of Cairo, is visited by millions of tourists.

Menkaura's pyramid
Here we see construction under way on the smallest of the three monumental pyramids at the Giza complex. Erected around 2490 BC, Menkaura's pyramid is only about 220 feet high with a base of 350 by 350 feet. Some original facing in granite is still visible in spite of the removal of most of the slabs over the centuries.

Khepri's pyramid
Dating to 2520 BC, this construction is 450 feet high with a base measuring 690 by 690 feet. The original facing in slabs of limestone can still be seen at the top.

Great Pyramid
This pyramid was built around 2550 BC by Khufu, the second pharaoh of the Fourth Dynasty. Almost two and a half million blocks of hard limestone were used, each one weighing about two and a half tons. The apex is just a few yards higher than Khepri's pyramid.

Building the pyramids
Even today it is difficult to imagine how the Egyptians built the pyramids. There are several theories about the kind of ramps used, but each hypothesis has met with objections. The secret of how the Egyptians moved and raised such enormous stones is still shrouded in mystery.

Three small pyramids
Here the three most important wives of the pharaoh Khufu are buried.

Ceremonial boat
An important part of the funeral ceremony was carrying the boat containing the pharaoh's body inside the pyramid. It was believed that the boat would take the pharaoh to rejoin the sun.

Measurements and orientation
The Great Pyramid is over 480 feet high and its point forms a 51.5 degree angle. Like the other pyramids, its sides are oriented toward the four cardinal points and its edges represent the sun's rays shining down on earth.

Sarcophagus
Once the processes of embalmment and wrapping were completed, the mummy was sealed inside the sarcophagus. This was considered the moment of the real funeral.

Ceremonial boat
Funerary vessels were constructed in a special shape that recalled the boat used by the sun god during his trip to the underworld. The pharaoh's body was placed under the canopy.

Procession
Priests shaved their heads to ensure perfect bodily hygiene.

Funerary complex
The pyramid complex consisted of two connecting temples. Overlooking the Nile, the first temple was where the pharaoh's body was embalmed. Afterwards priests led a long procession to carry the body to the funerary temple, next to the pyramid, where they performed sacred rites.

Great Sphinx
Carved from a large outcropping of limestone, this figure has the body of a crouching lion and the face of a king, probably Khepri.

Temple
Standing guard at the foot of the easternmost end of the Giza funerary complex, the Sphinx is considered part of the Khepri Valley temple.

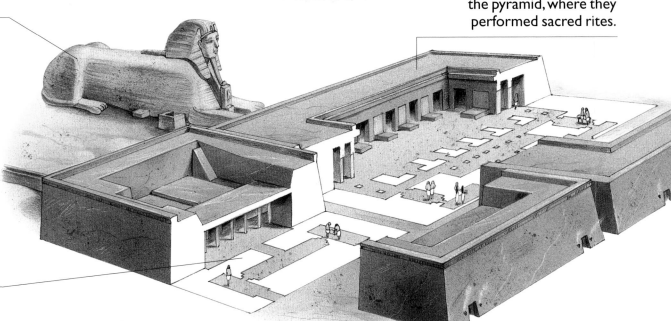

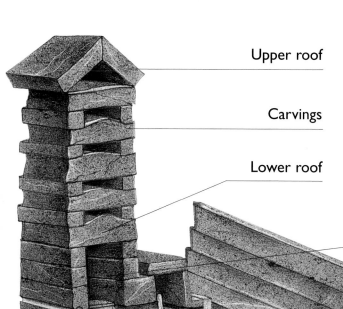

Upper roof

Carvings

Lower roof

The chamber where the pharaoh was buried.

Sarcophagus

Access corridor

Granite cover

The first coffin was made of wood covered with gilded plaster.

The second coffin of gilded wood was wrapped in a shroud.

The sarcophagus containing all the coffins was carved from quarz.

Funerary artifacts
Sealed in the tomb, the pharaoh's body was surrounded by personal items and everyday objects. It was believed they were useful to him during his afterlife.

Mummification
After cutting open one side of the body to extract the entrails, the cadaver was immersed in natural saltpeter before being treated with ointments and resins to make the skin supple.

Wrapping
After embalming, the next step was to wrap the body in linen bandages to protect it from external factors.

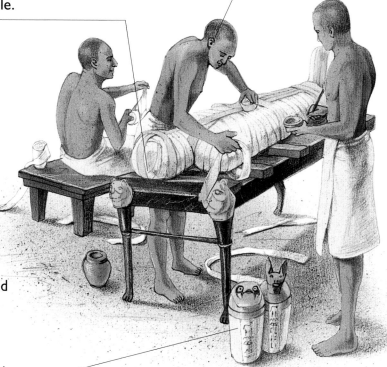

Furnishings
In some perfectly preserved tombs, archeologists have found chairs, beds, small tables, and benches, as well as objects for personal care like wigs, clothes, linens, and even food.

Canopic jars
Organs extracted from the body were treated separately and preserved in special "canopic" jars. Each organ was believed to be protected by a different funerary god.

THE GREAT PYRAMID

For 2 players

Object of the game:

To build the Great Pyramid, raising more stones than the other player

You will need:

3 dice
21 small tokens or coins

How to play:

The player who best imitates the Sphinx begins.

The Great Pyramid is divided into six levels numbered from 1 (at the bottom) to 6 (at the top). On his or her turn each player rolls and starts to place the first "stones" (the coins or tokens) at the base of the pyramid according to the number of dice rolled that show the number 1.

For example: On his or her turn a player rolls 1-3-5. With this roll he or she can place one token on one of the "stones" marked with a 1 at the bottom of the pyramid.

In order to remember whose coins are whose, one player will use only "heads" and the other only "tails." After his or her roll and any placement of the first "stones," the player passes the dice to the other player to begin his or her turn.

BE CAREFUL: You can't raise a stone to a new level without having two blocks to support it below–otherwise the whole structure will collapse! This is the reason why, to put a stone on the next level, you must already have two adjacent stones on the level below.

When a player succeeds in placing a stone on a higher level, he or she turns the two coins underneath to his or her side.

End of the game:

When the pyramid is completed and the last stone placed at the top, all the coins are counted to show to how many "heads" and how many "tails" were used. Whoever has more coins wins.

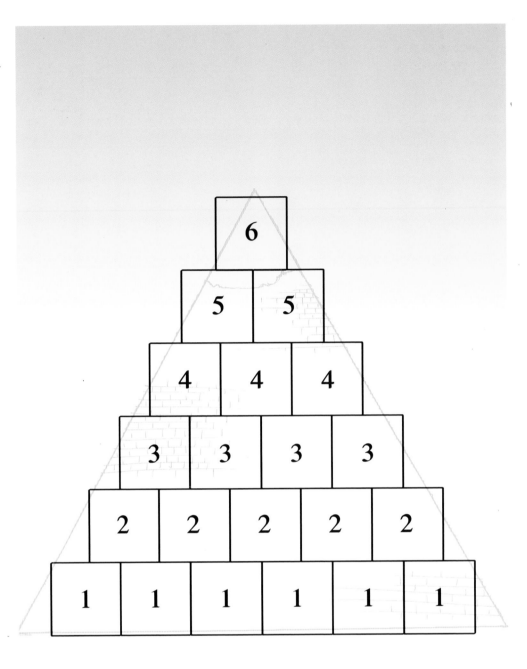

Dwellings
There was no distinction between rich and poor areas. Houses were built as one or more stories with terraced roofs; the windows, barred with wooden gratings, were little more than holes for letting in air.

Streets
They were as narrow and crowded as in any village.

A CAPITAL

Far south of Memphis, the city consecrated to the god Amun reached its greatest splendor during the New Kingdom (1550–1070 BC). Famous pharaohs like Tutankhamen reigned in this period. The city is remembered in history with its biblical name: Thebes.

At the market
Every day at the market people bartered for produce from the countryside, fish from the Nile, and livestock.

THE TEMPLE

During the New Kingdom, religious rites took place in great temples composed of courtyards, porticos, and chambers considered to be the dwelling places of gods.

The temple was at the center of a larger complex of buildings where gods and pharaohs lived together. The layout was always the same because, it was said, the rule had been established by the gods themselves. Temples also retained vast tracts of land, often tax exempt, where grain, fruit, and vegetables were cultivated.

Officiants
The pharaoh, as high priest, would have had to officiate in all the temples in Egypt, but his functions were usually carried out by the head priest. In the great temples, this man had enormous power and controlled the fabulous riches that made up the temple's treasure.

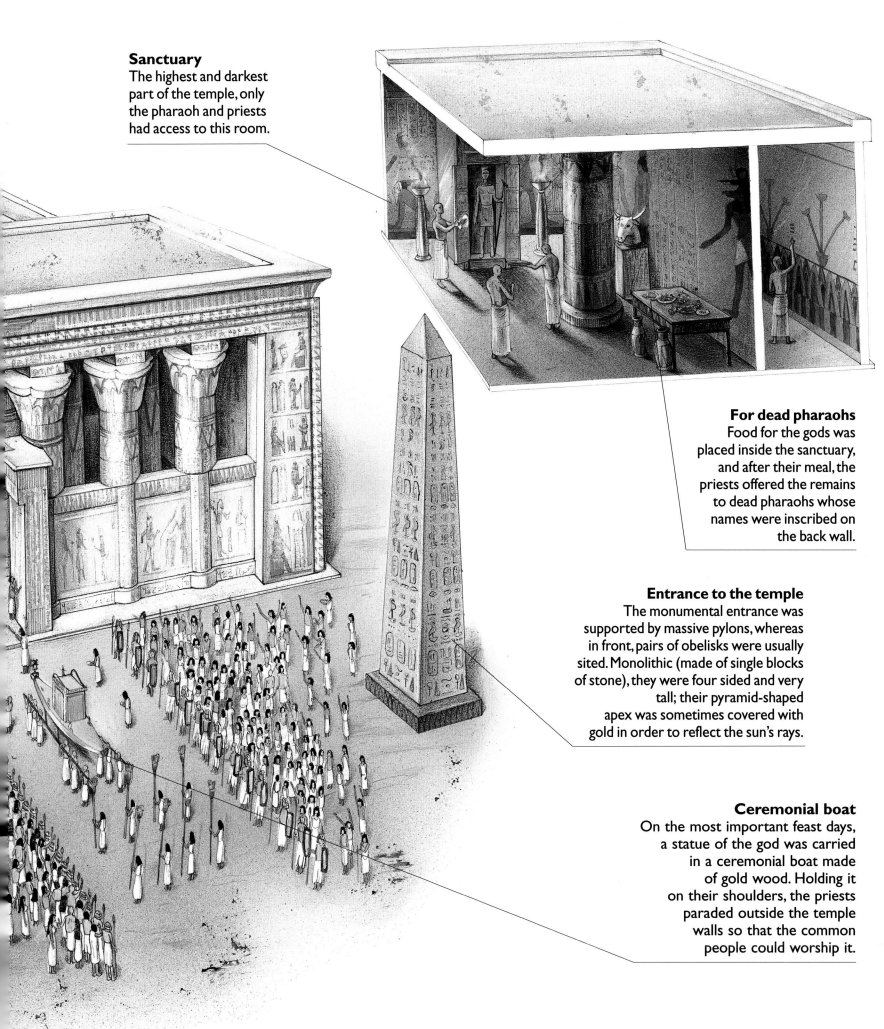

Sanctuary
The highest and darkest part of the temple, only the pharaoh and priests had access to this room.

For dead pharaohs
Food for the gods was placed inside the sanctuary, and after their meal, the priests offered the remains to dead pharaohs whose names were inscribed on the back wall.

Entrance to the temple
The monumental entrance was supported by massive pylons, whereas in front, pairs of obelisks were usually sited. Monolithic (made of single blocks of stone), they were four sided and very tall; their pyramid-shaped apex was sometimes covered with gold in order to reflect the sun's rays.

Ceremonial boat
On the most important feast days, a statue of the god was carried in a ceremonial boat made of gold wood. Holding it on their shoulders, the priests paraded outside the temple walls so that the common people could worship it.

GETTING TO KNOW MORE

PTOLMYS

ΠΤΟΛΕΜΑΙΟΣ

PTOLEMAIOS

From the Greek form of Ptolomy's name, Champollion was able to identify its hieroglyph equivalent; from there he set about trying to decipher the mysterious Egyptian writing. Hieroglyphs are figures that represent people and the world around them (plants, animals, etc.). Originally each sign was used as a pictogram: it portrayed its meaning (that is, the drawing of an owl meant "owl"), but over time the need to express abstract ideas and proper names resulted in the use of signs for their phonetic value, that is, as sounds.

What Is Egyptology?

Egyptology is the science that studies ancient Egyptian civilization from its origins to the fourth century AD (the period of the last known piece of hieroglyphic writing). After that time the meaning of hieroglyphic signs became lost and remained incomprehensible for many centuries. A decisive discovery was made in 1799, when, during Napoleon's military campaign in Egypt, French soldiers discovered the Rosetta stone, inscribed with three different languages: hieroglyphs, demotic, and Greek. Thanks to this find, the French scholar Jean-François Champollion was able, in 1822, to decipher the mysterious hieroglyphs. The discovery of the Rosetta stone and the key to decoding the language marked the beginning of modern Egyptology; the later study of excavation artifacts led to attempts to reconstruct the history and culture of a civilization that, until that time, had been completely unknown.

Origins of Egyptian Civilization

Egyptian civilization originated in Africa at the end of the fourth millennium BC Around that time some farming and herding peoples of central-north Africa settled in the Nile flood valleys because the once fertile and green Sahara area no longer guaranteed conditions for survival. Establishing agriculture in the Nile Valley required the combined efforts of many and more organized communities. Under the authority of the most important village, small communities grew up, each recognizing the power of one chief: this was the origin of the "pharoah" civilization.

The early settlements fought among themselves until, sometime around 3200 BC, in what is known as the Predynastic period, Egypt was divided into just two states. Around 3000 BC Narmer, the king of Upper Egypt, conquered Lower Egypt, unifying the country and starting the reign of 30 pharaoh dynasties.

The History of Egypt Under the Pharaohs

Scholars usually divide Egypt's long history (almost 3,000 years) into different eras: Old Kingdom (2649–2150 BC), First Intermediate period, Middle Kingdom (2130–1640 BC), Second Intermediate period, New Kingdom (1550–1070 BC), Third Intermediate period, Late period (1069–332 BC).

The Old Kingdom witnessed the establishment and definition of those political and social institutions to which the Egyptians would faithfully adhere for over 20 centuries.

Long isolated by the deserts surrounding them, the Egyptians were protected from enemy invasion and were almost never moved to attack other peoples. The pharaohs extended their dominion as far as Nubia to the south and exerted influence on Palestine to the east. The Egyptians were conquered by Alexander the Great in 332 BC.

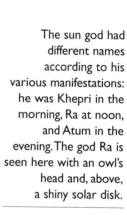

Of the many functionaries who represented the pharaoh's power, only the scribes learned to write the complicted Egyptian hieroglyphs. Scribes could be found in all the administrative offices; in the fields to survey land, count livestock, or weigh crops; at borders to check the traffic of foreigners and goods; and everywhere to collect taxes.

The Pharaohs

The first two dynasties, including the one founded by Narmer, belong to the Predynastic period, immediately preceeding the so-called Old Kingdom. More than 100 pharaohs ruled over Egypt, of whom the longest lived was Pepi II (VI dynasty), who ruled from 2278 to 2184 BC.

In ancient Egypt the pharaoh was at the top of the power structure, which one can visualize as a pyramid shape. He ruled over an estimated population of two to five million people, organized into provinces. Financial issues (taxes, tributes, production, etc.) were managed by the vizier, who was the highest functionary. He dealt with law and justice, so he was very powerful indeed. The vizier was aided by manangers responsible for main sectors—today we would call them a president's cabinet. They were the King's deputies and enforced his will through a network of lower functionaries and, on an even more local level, through provincial governors. At the bottom of the social ladder was a population estimated at about five million people during the New Kingdom, composed mostly of farmers.

Symbol of the state, the pharaoh also played an important role in religious affairs. As the incarnation of Maat, the goddess of order and justice, it was the pharaoh who guaranteed coherence and happiness for his country. Detainer of magic powers, mediator between earth and sky, he had to keep harmony between people and gods through his performance of religious rites in the temples.

Considered superior beings, the many Egyptian gods governed world affairs by their moods. At the top of the divine hierarchy was the sun god Atum, who had ordered the world from its primordial chaos. His offspring Isis and Osiris were very popular in the culture and were later worshiped by Greeks and Romans as well. The Egyptians believed that at sunset, the sun god was overpowered by shadows only to rise, triumphant, the next day. This was held up as proof of the soul's continuity after death, but to achieve this, an intact body was needed. This is the belief underlying the Egyptians' development of mummification, burial rites, and tomb construction.

The sun god had different names according to his various manifestations: he was Khepri in the morning, Ra at noon, and Atum in the evening. The god Ra is seen here with an owl's head and, above, a shiny solar disk.